THIS IS ME!

RHYTHMS OF LAUGHTER

Edited By Briony Kearney

First published in Great Britain in 2024 by:

Young Writers
Remus House
Coltsfoot Drive
Peterborough
PE2 9BF
Telephone: 01733 890066
Website: www.youngwriters.co.uk

Book Design by Ashley Janson

Softback ISBN 978-1-83565-336-4

Printed and bound in the UK by BookPrintingUK
Website: www.bookprintinguk.com
YB0MA0046A

FOREWORD

For Young Writers' latest competition This Is Me, we asked primary school pupils to look inside themselves, to think about what makes them unique, and then write a poem about it! They rose to the challenge magnificently and the result is this fantastic collection of poems in a variety of poetic styles.

Here at Young Writers our aim is to encourage creativity in children and to inspire a love of the written word, so it's great to get such an amazing response, with some absolutely fantastic poems. It's important for children to focus on and celebrate themselves and this competition allowed them to write freely and honestly, celebrating what makes them great, expressing their hopes and fears, or simply writing about their favourite things. This Is Me gave them the power of words. The result is a collection of inspirational and moving poems that also showcase their creativity and writing ability.

I'd like to congratulate all the young poets in this anthology, I hope this inspires them to continue with their creative writing.

CONTENTS

THE POEMS

Learning Is Fun!

Learning, learning is so fun,
It is good for everyone,
With this knowledge, you can grow,
To keep you like a pro,
Your brain gets stronger,
And won't be stopped by laziness any longer,
Science is the best,
Better than the rest,
You should do maths, you really should,
As for me, it is quite good,
History is cool,
Just remember, the Romans didn't always rule,
English is a breeze as it gives a lot of ease,
Be the best you can be,
Try to be just like me!

Abdullah Khan (9)

Lucky Mucky's Life

Lucky Mucky is white,
He loves to eat cookies.
Lucky Mucky has one sister,
Her name is Penny.
Lucky Mucky is lucky
Because he found ten pounds.
Coming back from monster school,
Lucky Mucky's dad lives far away.
But Lucky Mucky and his sister
Live with their mama.
In monster school he is quiet
But when he gets home
He talks to his sister and plays with her.

Holly McConville (9)

This Is Me

A m I a bit crazy, maybe?
N ever would I be naughty,
G orgeous and fun am I,
E legant with ballet,
L ikely to be a dancer when I grow up,
R oses are my favourite flower,
O ranges are my favourite fruit,
S unny days, I play on my swings,
E ventually, I will get a new trampoline.

Angelrose Johnson

This Is Me

S illy in drama with Lilly,
C ool in my flared jeans,
A rtistic,
R easonably tall-ish for my age,
L oyal to my friends,
E verlasting (not) love for my Vans bag,
T respass coats I hope I'll never wear,
T racy Beaker books are great (totally!).

Scarlett Johnson

Ibrahim

I play games on the PC
B lueberries taste good
R unning is fun and fast
A nd holidays are beautiful
H ot chicken is delicious
I sleep in bed to get my energy
M elons are also a good fruit.

Ibrahim Bahakam

This Is Me

Today, the clouds are grey,
I wish I could go out and play,
The rain patters and falls as fast as a cheetah
I feel blue, what can I do?

Anish Thakrar (7)

Fortnite

F irst game ever
O verpowered weapons
R age quitting
T ry harder
N o teaming
I n the vault looting
T eaming up in solos is bad
E veryone is good.

Eric Dinu (10)
Alexander Peden Primary School And Nursery, Harthill

Star Wars

I am a Jedi
I have a blue lightsaber
I live in a spaceship
I am brave
I am tall
I live in space
Who am I?

Answer: Obi-Wan Kenobi.

Alfie Brown (10)
Alexander Peden Primary School And Nursery, Harthill

This Is Me

I love my family
They make me feel loved and happy
I have a dog called Oakley
When we go for walks he comes back muddy

I love to go golfing and play rugby
This probably isn't the nicest-sounding melody
I love pizza and s'mores galore
Whenever I get them, I ask for more.

Ollie Fuller (11)
Bervie School, Montrose

This Is Me

My name is Riley and I love my dog,
I love playing with my dog in the woods with my family
Like my mam, my brothers and sister
But sometimes it is my dad and I but it's still fun.
I love my dad, he is my hero
And I love him so much.
This is me.

Riley Yates (11)
Bloemfontein Primary School, Craghead

This Is Me!

E xtraordinary
L unatic
E xtra
A mazing
N ot cool ice
O ver the top
R eally crazy

W eird
H appy
O h dear, Eleanor's here
M armoset lover
E cstatic
S uper duper.

Eleanor Whomes (9)
Bracken Leas Primary School, Brackley

Wacky Poem

Roses are red, violets are blue
And that's what gives me the flu.
Oranges are orange, blueberries are blue
And that's what makes me too.
Bees are yellow, bees are black
And if you come back I will give you a whack.
Yellow is yellow, so is a giraffe
And that's why I love giraffes.
Normal is me, normal is you
From that view
Nothing is nasty, nothing is true.

Robynn Purves (8)
Carnegie Primary School, Dunfermline

This Is Me

The Pars are one of the best teams in Scotland,
At one of the Pars games you will hear me roar!
"The Pars!"
Rocco is good,
But sometimes crazy,
Rocco is my dog if you didn't know,
I have best friends,
Colby, Albie, Jacob and I play video games,
My favourite is EA FC 24.

Cason Tate (9)
Carnegie Primary School, Dunfermline

Edan

I like playing football under the waterfall
And I have a dog that goes on blogs.
I played with Lego in San Diego.
I eat pizza rolls on the Japanese patrols.
I live in Scotland where there are salty seas.
My fave colour is blue, that's why it's on my shoe.

Edan Sandu (9)
Carnegie Primary School, Dunfermline

This Is Me

G reat at horse care and riding
E pic at football
O ptimistic and kind
R avenous all the time
G ood at creative writing
I ntelligent and a keen learner
A wesome dog owner

R eally funny, weird and crazy
O bedient learner
B rilliant believer in positivity
I like to win
N etball star
S pecial and unique
O n Apache, my world best pony ever
N ever on time.

Georgia Robinson (11)
Caversham Preparatory School, Caversham

This Is Me Recipe Poem

I nterestingly unique and special
N umerical ability is extremely large
C reative arts is my speciality
R eady for anything
E pic at most things
D rastically fierce
I ntelligence is a shining quality of mine
B elieve my life is winning
L earning is cool
E verything in the world is good

Z ara is amazingly kind
A wesomeness is insane
R oyal spark
A mazing at netball

N umbers are my thing
O bservant
E xtremely cool
L a, la, la, la, la!
L oving books
A t my A game.

Zara Kasozi (11)
Caversham Preparatory School, Caversham

This Is Me

T he world is special to me.
H aving family around me is what makes life glow.
I n life, I am grateful for what I have.
S aying kind words will put a friendly smile on somebody's face.

I am intelligent but will always want to be bright while learning.
S inging is what I love and will never stop loving it.

M indful and respectful towards others is who I am
E mily is who I am and would not have it any other way!

Emily Armaghanian (10)
Caversham Preparatory School, Caversham

I Am Raphael

I ntelligent in mathematics but struggle in English

A mazing with playing video games
M ysterious when I'm playing in the snow

R adical at playing rugby
A wesome at times tables
P rofessional when I'm doing my drama
H ilariously great at woodwork
A mbitious when I'm doing my work
E xcited about Christmas
L ooking out for people who might be hurt.

Raphael Roughneen (11)
Caversham Preparatory School, Caversham

This Is Me

I maginative at thinking of stories

A mbitious and hard-working
M agnificent at playing instruments

L ovely and kind
U nique than other people
C reative
Y eti lover

W eird and wacky

Y orkshire pudding eater.

Lucy Warren-Yeo (10)
Caversham Preparatory School, Caversham

This Is Me

I 'm bad at sports but getting better

A lways trying to be the best I can
M arvellous at making Lego sets

G ood at story writing
I ncredible at tennis but have space to improve
A lways trying to be positive
N aughty some of the time.

Gian Mattu (10)
Caversham Preparatory School, Caversham

This Is Me

I am good at sport

Amazing personality
Motors make me excited

Origami is not my thing
Socialising is what I'm amazing at
Colours are my weird art
Always kind but fun
Running makes me tired.

Oscar Wright (10)
Caversham Preparatory School, Caversham

This Is Me!

T homas
H appy and humorous
I ntelligent
S tylish

I nteresting
S ing like an out-of-tune violin

M eat eater
E xecutive.

Thomas Willenbrock (9)
Caversham Preparatory School, Caversham

Me

Gather vanilla and kindness,
A pinch of sugar,
Put in a bowl and stir in love for parents.
Pour in some chocolate milk,
Season with dance and gymnastics.
Now blend silliness and smartness.
Lastly, put in the fridge for seven hours.

Amelia Kalinowska (10)
Elmvale Primary School, Springburn

All About Me

L ovely friend
E legant
e **X** tra helpful
I love Harry Potter

F riendly and fancy
A mazing
W orks hard always
K ind
E pic
S uper sweet.

Lexi Fawkes (10)
Elmvale Primary School, Springburn

All About Sarah

S uper kind
A mazing at everything
R eally loves the colours of the rainbow
A lways loving to others and shares kindness
H as a heart of gold.

Sarah Duncan (10)
Elmvale Primary School, Springburn

All About Me

My name is Ridhima,
My best friend is Amila.
She is beautiful, you have to see her.
And I am gorgeous too, like a pretty girl.

Ridhima Manwar (9)
Elmvale Primary School, Springburn

A Recipe For Toby

First, gather some cuteness and cuddles.
Stir in some string and cat food.
Season with some magic fur.
Add a pinch of meowing.
Pour in a cup of curiosity.
And a touch of tiredness.
Blend dogs and cats, mice and rats.
Then warm gently by having fun and there you have it... my Toby Tots.

Lucas Easeman (9)
Gorsewood Primary School, Runcorn

Purple

P urple
U nited Kingdom
R ocks
P rime we have
L ots of Prime
E ats chocolates.

Ajay Pixton (9)
Hazel Grove Primary School, Stockport

My Life

S o, I love axolotls a lot and mine has
A hammock, also I am a boy, not a girl. My
M um looked up what an axolotl's favourite food
is and it is bloodworms. I love Pokémon. I am

G iga Hamster (it's a joke). Also, I'm a bad poet,
R ubbish (I think) and I am not used to poems.
O nce, I might have done a good poem and I
named it
'V -Times'. I hope I do good. I am nervous. Anyway,
E very day, I get excited for
S leep.

Sam Groves (9)
Heron Hill Primary School, Kendal

All About Me Poem

L ives in Kendal
U nited Kingdom is my favourite country
K etchup is my favourite sauce
E nvironment is amazing

M y eyes are blue
A pples and bananas are my favourite fruit
S wimming is my favourite sport
O ak trees are my favourite trees
N ettles are my least favourite plant.

Luke Mason (10)
Heron Hill Primary School, Kendal

This Is Me!

First, gather a sharp pencil and a drawing book.
Stir in golf clubs and some golf balls.
Season with fun.
Add a pinch of basketball.
Pour in football
And dogs.
Blend toy guns and drawing.
Then warm gently with me.

Lewis (9)
Heron Hill Primary School, Kendal

Hi, My Name Is Christian

Hi, my name is Christian
I really like chicken nuggets.
Computing, I do it every day
Pokémon, dragons, I love both.
I have rollerskates, a bike, also a pogo stick
An Xbox S, so I'm pretty happy.

Christian Hope (9)
Heron Hill Primary School, Kendal

This Is Me

Pizza is always cheesy
Hot and yummy
If you don't like vegetables
That are on pizzas
Just have a bite
Because pizzas are always cheesy
Hot and yummy.

Tanvi Verma
Khalsa (VA) Primary School, Southall

I Am Me

I am the sun, patiently waiting to arise for a new day
With beautifully designed beds below and beside me
Waking up and getting ready for school
Going outside, walking, feeling happy and free

Going into the classroom reading a book called The Escape
Asking myself questions, reading about challenges that await
Starting with the subject of reading
And ending with the subject of PSHE, Science or History

With the hope of one day becoming a doctor
Going home and playing with my younger brother
When I let myself down, he allows me to rise
Being honest with myself and others around me

But at the end of the day, I go to bed
Pondering what will happen next
Before going to bed, I think to myself
I am David, I am me.

David Afonso (11)
Kingfisher Hall Primary Academy, Enfield

This Is Me

The month that I was born,
Months and months I waited,
Just to celebrate the day I was born,
23rd of September, to be exact,
It's the day my parents lit my candle with a match.

My hobbies outside of school,
Gold, silver, bronze, it doesn't matter, at least I tried my best,
Me and myself will always get stuck but we always find a solution,
Fighting and defending is hard, but learning is extreme,
Battle IQ is all you need, and points are all you need to win.

My hobbies inside of school,
Swishing and splashing are all I need to be a better version of myself,
Running and jumping is what I do,
Being a captain brings out the best version of everyone,
Smaller or taller, it doesn't matter, it's how you play ball.

My favourite subjects in school,
Numbers and calculation are what I like,
The past is understandable, but the future is unknown,
Styles of art describe you,
New objects or living things are still a mystery in life.

My goals in life,
Bronze, silver; next, it's gold for the victory,
100% attendance at school increases knowledge and knowledge is power,
After 21 points, try till you reach your limits and score even more baskets!

Adam Emambacus (11)
Kingfisher Hall Primary Academy, Enfield

My Emotion

Thinking about cake,
I can't have it,
I have a wheat allergy,
Tasting wheat and cake in my mouth,
Wanting to eat it,
Now all I want is food,
Soon it will be snack time,
Then I can have some food.

Jane Skinner (9)
Kingfisher Primary School, Houndstone

Family Is Good

F amily cares for you.
A n older brother or sister may tell you off but only to benefit you.
M y family is the best.
I love my family.
L ove and don't shout at your parents.
Y ou should be grateful to have your family.

I have a perfect family.
S adly, sometimes they get really angry.

G ood is what your family should be, they should be excellent.
O ne life is all you have with them.
O bviously, make it count.
D o you love your family? I do.

Muhammad Yusuf Shikora (10)
Lammack Primary School, Blackburn

This Is Me

T houghtful - showing consideration for other people
H elpful - helping others
I nspirational - showing creative or spiritual inspiration
S uccessful - someone who has achieved something in life.

I ntelligent - someone who is really smart
S mart - someone who knows quite a lot of things.

M indful - someone who thinks
E ntertaining - someone who entertains people.

This is me!

Amaani Hussain (9)
Lammack Primary School, Blackburn

This Is Me

I am Umar, this is me.
I love bikes, scooters, anything with wheels.
I'm a professional biker and I learned it one to two years ago.
I had a 3x3, I popped, I snapped.
I also had a 2x2 which my sister broke and a 4x4 which I still have.

Umar Paxel (9)
Lammack Primary School, Blackburn

Liverpool

L ively in the stadium,
I n the field, Mo's the man,
V ideographers love the game,
E ven before LFC, Klopp was the man,
R ed is the colour of the best,
P icking up the ball, Alisson is the man,
O ver his head,
O n the ball, Trent is the man,
L iverpool is here for the treble and nothing less.

Logan Mauchart-Williams (11)
North Crescent Primary School, Wickford

What Am I?

I'm very funky,
But not a monkey,
I like climbing up a tree,
I'm not a bee,
You'll see me running with my mates,
Even on dates,
I like nuts,
But not living in huts.
What am I?

Answer: A chipmunk.

Sienna Skeat (10)
North Crescent Primary School, Wickford

This Is Me, Theresa

T eacher helps me with my work.
H ating my little brother's cry.
E njoying learning from my teacher.
R eading my book.
E ating food.
S easide is my favourite thing
A nd by my little brothers.

Theresa Ellis (8)
North Crescent Primary School, Wickford

Samuel Poem

S uper-duper good at sports
A nd plays for a football team.
M is for me, I have brown hair.
U nderstands and sometimes doesn't.
E asygoing and loves maths.
L oves school and loves food.

Samuel Grote (10)
North Crescent Primary School, Wickford

Divine

D reaming about Asda.
I am Divine and I like going to Costco.
V aluing other people.
I love Minecraft.
N o, I don't like bees.
E njoying going to Tesco.

Divine Gyebi (8)
North Crescent Primary School, Wickford

Bridget Poem

B - I have brown hair
R eady for things
I love ice cream
D odgeball is fun
G ood at having no friends
E at all the time
T errific at being kind.

Bridget Mcdonagh (9)
North Crescent Primary School, Wickford

This Is Me, Archie

A nimals are my favourite
R eading books
C ats are my favourite animal
H ungry for McDonald's
I like going to the slide
E njoying reading.

Archie Mccann (7)
North Crescent Primary School, Wickford

This Is Me, Louie

L ooking cool
O verexcited when playing with my friends
U p and out of my bed at the beginning of the day.
I love doughnuts.
E mbracing my mum is lovely.

Louie Barter (7)
North Crescent Primary School, Wickford

This Is Me, Dolly

D ancing with my sisters is fun.
O utside play is fantastic.
L ove to sing.
L ike to play with my friends.
Y ellow and pink could be my favourite colours.

Dolly Skeat (8)
North Crescent Primary School, Wickford

This Is Me, Aria

A pples are my favourite fruit.
R eading is my favourite lesson.
I love being at school.
A nimals make me happy when I am upset.

Aria Williams (7)
North Crescent Primary School, Wickford

All About Me

I am Jasmine,
I have a friend called Yasmine
I am kind and respectful
Careful and special,
I like gymnastics,
And I'm fantastic.

Jasmine-Lilly Joyce (10)
North Crescent Primary School, Wickford

This Is Me, Paul

I like Pokémon.
I like trains.
I am a happy little boy.
I like gaming.
I love my family.
This is me, Paul.

Paul Hazelton (8)
North Crescent Primary School, Wickford

Will

Will
Smart and sporty,
Football lover forever,
Focused on the game
Will.

Will Sockett (9)
North Crescent Primary School, Wickford

How To Make Me

Ingredients:
One grain of sand
A hint of skill
One litre of cat lover potion
A teaspoon of style
A cup of creativity
A hint of skill
A handful of cool
A pinch of chattiness
A dash of flashy clothes
A heart full of joy and love

Method:
Find a cauldron and pour in one litre of cat lover potion.
Add in a dash of flashy clothes.
Toss in a handful of cool.
After that sprinkle in a teaspoon of style.
Throw in a cup of creativity.
Mix in a pinch of chattiness (in class).
Now a hint of skill will be added to the pot
As well as one grain of sand.

Finally, chuck in a heart full of joy and love.
And there you go... You just made me!
Now sit back and relax while I do fun activities with you.

Khadijah Mirza (8)

Oak Tree Primary School, Mitcham

All About Me

This is me
I'm a tough defender
I play professional games every time
I'm a dashing player
Aggressively injure people sometimes.

My school is Oak Tree Primary School
I play football every day
A competitive gamer
Play a lot
And read sometimes
Also, I'm a very calm and active person.

Who am I?
Now you know all about me!

Rehan Uddin (11)
Oak Tree Primary School, Mitcham

This Is Me!

T he beach is my favourite place to be
H ome is where I feel safe and comfortable
I am as funny as a joke
S chool keeps me brave and calm

I like to swim
S unday is my birthday

M y favourite colour is lilac
E verything about me is like Christmas. My hair is as red as Santa's hat. My eyes are as green as a Christmas tree.

Leyla Stirling (8)
Old Monkland Primary And Nursery School, Coatbridge

Magdalena City

M y name is a city, big and small
A puppy is all I need to cheer me up
G reat height for helping others
D iamond nose on my diary
A brother who is a greedy pig
L ove to collect L.O.L.s
E xperience bleeding way too much
N ovember is beautiful to me
A ll of this is me!

Magdalena Bochno (8)
Old Monkland Primary And Nursery School, Coatbridge

I Am Breanna

B aking is my favourite thing
R eaching for the sprinkles
E ating cakes is so much fun
A nd I put them in the oven
N ice and hot and fluffy
N utella toppings
A pple pie is nice and yummy.

Breanna Brown (8)
Old Monkland Primary And Nursery School, Coatbridge

I Am Jan

I love wooden toys

A irports are my favourite places
M aria is my younger sister

J an is my name
A eroplanes are my favourite to learn about
N ot really happy often.

Jan Amin-Luszczynski (9)
Old Monkland Primary And Nursery School, Coatbridge

All About Me

I love a reaction!
I'm always on the scene.
I like knowing what is going on.
I like to pretend I don't care
But I shrug my shoulders there and then.
I like cricket.

Charlie Izzard (9)
Oughton Primary & Nursery School, Hitchin

All About Me

I am Lewis
Loves maths
Eating sausages
My favourite food is hot dogs
Loves gaming
And helping my siblings
I am Lewis.

Lewis-Stanley Mowlem (9)
Oughton Primary & Nursery School, Hitchin

This Is Me!

I love to do backflips
But I love to eat chips.
I like roller coasters that do flips!
This is me!

Caison Mullings (9)
Oughton Primary & Nursery School, Hitchin

This Is Me

T all in size
H ave many good friends
I like swimming
S chool is the best

I am a rainbow of emotion
S chool is the best

M y name is Jason
E very day, me and my siblings and parents put
our hands together and clean the whole house.

Jason Echono (9)
Our Lady Catholic Primary School, Welwyn Garden City

I Am...

I am the handle of a paintbrush
Because I like art,
Allowing me to get away from the world.

I am the light of a candle
Because I'm so bright
And can make people's day.

I am the furriness of a chinchilla
Because I am soft,
Nice, kind and friendly.

I am the carer of a bed
Because I like sleeping
And dreaming in peace and quiet.

I am the water of the sea
Because I can go as far as I can,
Get away from all bad energy.

This is me.

Darcie-Fair Wood (10)
Parkview Primary School, Oakwood

My Favourite Colour Is Red!

Red makes me feel like a beautiful glimmering heart.
Red is a tasty, yummy strawberry.
Red feels like a big red, joyful petal.
Red is a relaxing taste.
Red roses that are happy make me feel bright.
I love everything about this!

Ryleigh Drew (7)
Parkview Primary School, Oakwood

Lily Dilly

My name is Lily and sometimes I am a bit silly.
My sister says I am very funny.
I also love apples with honey.
I love playing with Kinetic Sand.
I dream of being in a band.
I have a dog
But I don't like walking him in the fog.
His name is Loki
And he loves doing the hokey cokey!

Lily Southam (9)
Ravensden CE Primary Academy, Ravensden

My Favourite Things

The dolphins are playing in the sun, having lots of fun,
They're playing with a bouncy ball, having such fun.
They dance, they swim, they loop the loop,
Spraying water around the coop.
While on the beach with a drink, he slurps up the refreshing drink
Then walks to the shore to have a dip,
Sitting up in the remote coconut tree
While the green leaves sparkle or bananas perch between the tree putting on his speakers!
But on the shore oh look, oh look,
Mrs Penguin with the group,
They cheer, they scream and even steal an ice cream.
They run around making a noise,
Cursing avocado to enjoy.
They even throw an ice cream at Mrs Bungalo!
Mr Bungolo gets annoyed and wakes up Floyd,
Floyd is a massive crab that can eat people alive.
Who are bad!

It yawns, it grumbles, and gets up with a stumble,
It stops then stares and puts his massive slimy foot
on top of the penguin troup!

Dodo Tobin (10)
Repton Preparatory School, Milton

About Me

So you want to know about me...
Okay, so I was always afraid of not fitting in and all that.
My mum keeps telling me to dress how I want to.
And that I was always dressing how everyone was dressing (e.g. so wearing jeans, cargos, white shirts, oversized jumpers)...
So my mum told me to dress differently.
But I had a complete meltdown because of that, but in the end she won.
So I went to school wearing shorts, black tights and a white shirt.
I kept saying to her that people were going to call me an emo kid.
But when I got to school no one said anything so I felt okay.
Until some Year 8 came up to me I was so scared, but all they said was, "I like what you're wearing."

Pavla Vernik (10)
Repton Preparatory School, Milton

My Personality

I absolutely love football,
It's the sport I play.
I play usually, which is every day.
I play football, I play for an academy.
I play at school with my friends,
And now I'm really happy.
I have a family, my sister, my mum and dad.
My sister always does dancing and she gets very sad.
I have a dog, he is very big.
He loves to go outside, and likes to dig.
I have another member, it's my gran.
She loves going on holiday, but doesn't get a tan.
I play sports, I'm very fit.
I will turn up to school with the right kit.
This is me, I have lots of fun.
I have written this poem, now I'm done.

Harry Cullen (9)
Repton Preparatory School, Milton

This Is Me

Excellent at sport and being a friend.
I will never forget my friends until the end.
I am a dog kind of guy,
A bit like David Attenborough.
I am very nice and kind to others.
I also make people have a fun time
By making everyone laugh because I make a lot of jokes.
I am clever and mentally strong as well.
I am also very helpful and I also have a really nice family.
I am a boarder and miss them every day
Though I have to get on with it anyway.
I am a good friend and I am also very energetic in sport.
I am a very loyal, caring person
And I am very open-minded to my friends.

Ted Mack
Repton Preparatory School, Milton

All About Me And My School

I am Otto.
I love football and hockey because I'm brave and strong.
I love dogs because they make my life fun.
I love food because of the texture and sensation.
If you were my friend I would make fun.
I play with my friends, Zachary, Theo, Rufus and Ted.
If you were me you would be good at art at Repton you can't play darts!
But at Repton you will have fun
At home I can never dream of Bertie, Millie, Zac.
When I'm alone I chill and eat snacks till dawn.
Until I go to sleep which is a little bit irritating and devilish
If I do say so myself.

Otto de Lisle (9)
Repton Preparatory School, Milton

Me And Grandpa Spider-Man

I like playing with my grandpa.
I've had a very strange day,
I feel like I've gone astray.
Right, I'll start from the beginning...
When I was winning.
I went to my grandpa's house today,
Just to play,
But then I heard a ring,
From the telephone thing,
My grandpa just rushed out of the door,
Never like before.
Eventually, I found him in the backyard,
He dressed in a red suit,
He didn't look like a guard.
Then he stood and threw a little web and went to fly
But before he did it he ate a big pie.

Osian Mayling (9)
Repton Preparatory School, Milton

This Is Me

My name is Wilfred,
I am good at gymnastics,
I like being helpful
And I love doing art.
I have lots of amazing friends,
I also love doing really cool flips
And I am pretty fast.
I am a good climber,
I am also a brother to two great siblings
Who are sometimes like a phone alarm in the morning.
All of my friends call me Spider-Man
I also love doing maths.
I have two Jack Russells who are the cutest things in the world.
I am an animal guy but I don't like spiders too much because of their creepy legs.

Wilfred Cursham
Repton Preparatory School, Milton

Me

I'm Tom.
I like things like football, FIFA, cricket, cross country,
Athletics and many more.
I am going to talk about me, Tom Watson.
I have two brothers,
Max who is six and Freddie who is twelve.
My mum is Clair, who is forty-two
And Simon who is forty-four.
Then there's me, I am ten.
I live in Repton, Derbyshire in Fieldhouse.
My favourite thing is to play football,
I'm a left-wing, centre-mid and right-wing.
I support Notts Country.
Hopefully that's all you need to know.

Tom Watson (10)
Repton Preparatory School, Milton

The Football Game Went Wrong

H appy when I have the ball
U sually I score
G lad to celebrate a goal
O ne goal, two goals, three goals, back of the net!

B eside the goal that was a fight.
A big punch hit me.
I froze with fear.
L eading the team I stopped the fight.
E ight people stopped fighting for me.
Y es! Everyone listened to me and now it's all happy.

Hugo Bailey (10)
Repton Preparatory School, Milton

Bright Side

Me... I am different, I'm not always the best
Sometimes I really just need a rest.
I can be ambitious most of the time,
Although those dreams just get crushed like kindling in the fire.
Sometimes people feel sympathy
Though they just don't know how it feels.
One day I could wake up and it all be a dream
But no, I wouldn't like that
Because every bad thing always has a bright side.

Magnus Lavery (10)
Repton Preparatory School, Milton

This Is Me

I am Pippa
I am kind and caring
I'm always here to help
I am happy, funny
And a sibling of three.

I love anything to do with sport
I am always filled with energy
I also think I am really good at sport
You will also find me with animals, I love them.

I'm a good friend and always fun
I think I am brilliant and special
This is me.

Pippa Major (9)
Repton Preparatory School, Milton

My Luxurious Life

I'm so athletic and some people even say I'm magnetic.
I'm also a dog lover and I'm undercover.
I'm also fit and I never quit.
I have a pus-filled sister, I want to pop her like a blister!
She sounds so much like Adolf Hitler.
I like McDonald's and I have a friend called Ronald.
I'm very good at football and I like throwing balls.

Sidney Croake (9)
Repton Preparatory School, Milton

Me

I like food
Chicken nuggets
I like food
I eat fruit
I eat chips
I like pasta and spaghetti
I am always in the mood
I like apples
I like mango
I like pineapple juice
I'm so brave
I'm so funny
I eat cake
I'm athletic
I am magic
I am kind
I am friendly
I am strong
I'm a gamer.

Theodore Sanders (9)
Repton Preparatory School, Milton

Ice Cream And Jelly

It's like you're in a dream
With ice cream, chocolate fountains and jelly,
Do not watch the telly.
But let's bring it up a notch.
This year is near to being good
With winter and a lot of mud.
It's near Christmas and reindeer antlers and lots of Santa.
With mistletoe and wine
You can hear the Christmas chimes.

Teddie Bird (10)
Repton Preparatory School, Milton

Rainbow

Red, yellow, blue and green
These are the colours that make up me!
I come in the sun, I come in the rain,
Maybe you can start to see who I am.
There is a myth that may be true
That pot at the end of me,
That pot is full of gold.
I hope you see who I am
Because that's the end of my poem.

Annie Thompson (10)
Repton Preparatory School, Milton

About Me!

Hugo is a little boy
A football is his favourite toy
At the weekend, he plays video games
And sometimes it is a video game pain.
"Game over."
I am cute,
Like a flute,
And I like to shoot in a football goal.
I am athletic and do track
Turkish Delight is my favourite snack.

Hugo Clayton (9)
Repton Preparatory School, Milton

I Have A Little Life

I have a little life
My name is Mollie and I am very mucky
I have a sister and she is silly
I like spaghetti, it is very stringy
I like hockey, it is always hopeful
I love horse riding, it is wholesome and
I like sports, I love to be sporty.

Mollie Sayers (9)
Repton Preparatory School, Milton

This Is Me

I'm a great gamer,
I love gaming, especially Pokémon games.
I love dogs, mainly Snoodles and Schnauzers.
They make me happy.
I'm strong, brave, loyal, risk-taking,
Fit, helpful, respectful and smart.
I'm a human.

Rory Hatton
Repton Preparatory School, Milton

Me

O pen-minded
L ovely
I ndependent
V ery clever
E asy-going
R esponsible

H ysterical
U ngovernable
N ever scared
T enacious.

Oliver Hunt
Repton Preparatory School, Milton

Me

A dash of my favourite foods
A sprinkle of my friends
Add a little English and art for a fabulous touch
A hint of my style
A pinch of my personality
Makes a lovely bake called... Me!

Grace Hanson (10)
Repton Preparatory School, Milton

My Dogs

I have a big dog and a little dog.
I have a loud dog and a quiet dog.
I have a cuddly dog and a distant dog.
I have a sleepy dog and an energetic dog.
These dogs are my dogs.

Quinn Goodall (10)
Repton Preparatory School, Milton

The World's Cans And Can'ts

I am Daniel
I am a human, not a Spaniel
You want to know more about me?
You want to hug me?
Well, that can never be!
You want to be a bee?
Well, that can never be!

Daniel Presland (9)
Repton Preparatory School, Milton

If I'm A...

Haiku poetry

If I'm a colour,
Shy at first, then bright and loud,
I would be yellow.

If I'm a season,
Rain or shine, I'll be happy,
Summer it will be.

Gia Kang-Mor (11)
Repton Preparatory School, Milton

Never Give Up

Be yourself,
Never give up,
Don't listen to anyone except yourself,
Be strong,
Keep on going,
Be your best,
Go far,
Do what's best.

Kuba Dawson (10)
Repton Preparatory School, Milton

This Is Me!

I am...
Fearless,
Adventurous,
Brave,
Happy,
Proud,
Wonderful.

That is me!

Kaeden Singh (8)
Repton Preparatory School, Milton

Football Is The GOAT

Football is the GOAT!
You can play football on a boat
It is cold outside
So play it in a coat.

Talha Mohammed (10)
Repton Preparatory School, Milton

This Is Me

Sport is my hobby
Gorillas are my favourite animal
I'm messy like a bird's nest.

Phoebe Reeves (9)
Repton Preparatory School, Milton

Me

To make me you will need:
A teaspoon of kindness
A jug of Taylor Swift
A splash of swimming
4 cups of cheekiness
1 ginormous spoon of arts and crafts
2 cats called Poppy and Tulip

Instructions:
First, get a spoon and a spatula
Mix in a teaspoon of kindness with 4 cups of cheekiness
Then throw in a jug of Taylor Swift
Now mix all together
Put in the oven for 35 minutes at 90°F
Now for the topping
A splash of swimming with one ginormous, spoon of arts and crafts
And last, but not least, 6 teaspoons of two cats called Poppy and Tulip
Mix thoroughly till a light, fluffy colour

Get a spatula and get all the excess out of the bowl
Now spread on the cake
Enjoy!

Isabelle McCann (10)

RGS Dodderhill School, Droitwich Spa

Recipe For Me!

First, you need to get a baking tray
Then get a large bowl

Ingredients:
A teaspoon of Christmas
A hint of slime
A pinch of fashion
A spoonful of art

Put that all in the bowl and give it a proper mix
Put it in the oven for ten minutes
Icing time! First, let it cool for three minutes
To put the put icing on, you need a sprinkle of black kittens
And a cruise around Barbados and Mauritius
Pipe it on
Last of all, a sprinkle of my family
Enjoy!

Imogen McCann (10)
RGS Dodderhill School, Droitwich Spa

Nature

N is for nature and all the wildlife we see
A is for the amazing plants, bright and lovely
T is for the terrific trees, tall and green
U is for the most unbelievable scenery I've ever seen
R is for the rainbows and rosey red sunsets too
E is for the extreme climate change affecting me and you.

Amarah Bedi (9)
RGS Dodderhill School, Droitwich Spa

This Is Me

T he best thing in my life is my family and my pets (Nacho, Pepper, Luna, Floyd, Bella, Trix, Bob and Mini!)
H eather is my sister
I love my cousins, KK and Misha, they are the best
S easide at my grandma's is the best

I love my life
S ometimes I get annoyed

M e and my friends love going to the park behind my house
E njoying watching movies with my cousins is my favourite thing to do!

Violet Simmons (10)
St Bede's Catholic Junior School, Appleton Village

My Silliness

The silliness inside me is as daft as a clown.
It's as loud as a lion;
As powerful as a punch.
It laughs and tickles and giggles and pokes.
It always escapes, then escapes again.
It often helps me to build friendships and bring people joy;
Sometimes, it will get me into trouble and make me laugh until it hurts.
There are many moments when I wish
It would simply let me be,
Yet my silliness is here to stay
For ever and eternity.

Rhys Sparks (10)
St Bede's Catholic Junior School, Appleton Village

Recipe Of Me!

Take a splash of moonlight and a hint of stars
A pinch of my parrot, Pickford
Get a handful of Simba's hair
And give Nala the spins by spinning her round six times
Crack in a song by BTS
Then add my aunty and cousins because they are the best
Fold in The Greatest Showman, Harry Potter and Fantastic Beasts
Roll it out thinly and sprinkle on some fun!
This is me!

Abi Mellor (11)
St Bede's Catholic Junior School, Appleton Village

This Is Me

Kind, amazing
A super hard worker
Maths is my superpower
History makes me suffer
I jump up and down
I sprint like a car
I'm a lifelong noodles fan
I'm sweet, I'm sour
I'm calm on one side
But crazy 24/7
So this is me
I am mostly happy, rarely sad
Always a good help
Loves to watch TV
I love my friends and family.

Kaiya Worsley (10)
St Bede's Catholic Junior School, Appleton Village

A Recipe To Be Me

You will need:
A house full of art
A pinch of kindness
10lb of joy
A room full of photography
A town of fashion designs
And finally, 100s of dogs

Method:
Mix the joy with the fashion and bake.
Then mix in the dogs.
Put everything in the cake and decorate.
Then you have me!

Aleia Martindale (10)
St Bede's Catholic Junior School, Appleton Village

This Is Me!

To create me you will need:
A cockapoo
A chocolate pizza
Some pink sprinkles
Fresh milk
Mix together and crumble over some Oreos
Stir in lots of sugar
Bake me for five minutes
Chill me in the fridge
Enjoy me at Christmas
My favourite time of the year!

Robbie Sutton (10)
St Bede's Catholic Junior School, Appleton Village

This Is Me

My name is Lucas
I am a superfast mind
English is my superpower
So I must be smart
I play football
I love art
So I am creative.
Here we go again
I love Pokémon
And any TV I can
I love my dog, Sandy
You have found out
About me!

Lucas Shaw (10)
St Bede's Catholic Junior School, Appleton Village

This Is Me

I am a...
Pokémon player
TV watcher
Hot dog eater
Cuddly toy lover
Prime drinker
Book reader
Dog walker
FNAF gamer
Snake lover
And finally...
Toast eater.

Jackson Edge (10)
St Bede's Catholic Junior School, Appleton Village

This Is Me

I am...
A great singer
A pizza maker
A 'Three of Us' watcher
A music listener
A good dancer
But most of all...
A good boy!

Dominic Woods (11)
St Bede's Catholic Junior School, Appleton Village

This Is Me

I am...
A good footballer
A hot dog eater
A Coca-Cola drinker
A YouTube watcher
A Prime drinker
And finally...
A good helper.

Sam Jones (10)
St Bede's Catholic Junior School, Appleton Village

Things I Like To Do

I like to...
Play soccer with my dad
Play fight with my sister but it never ends well
Box with my dad and both of my uncles
Go on holiday because I get two a year
Play table tennis with my dad
Play Fortnite with my friends and speak to
them too
Open my birthday and Christmas presents
Play football in and out of school
Play basketball with my sister and dad at home
Teach my little sister how to play online games
Play 'keep the balloon in the air' with my sister
and two step sisters.

Louis Goose (8)
St Mary's Catholic Voluntary Academy, Marple Bridge

This Is Me

I'm a good footballer
I like the piano
I love art
I'm a great swimmer
I love my three dogs
Two are super frogs
Jumping all over the world
I like chocolate but not milk or dark
I love Wales but we go too much
And this is me.

Thomas Henderson (10)
St Mary's Catholic Voluntary Academy, Marple Bridge

Lydia

L ying in the sun all relaxed on the ground
Y ou are a star in my eye
D rifting down a sunny stream
I n the meadow, you are like a butterfly
A nd you shine so bright like a star in the sky.

Florence Ferns (7)
St Mary's Catholic Voluntary Academy, Marple Bridge

This Is Me

I am a good brother
I am a good gamer
I am a good helper
I am a generous person
I am a fantastic footballer
I am a tall basketball player
I am an animal lover
This is me.

Theo Moores (8)
St Mary's Catholic Voluntary Academy, Marple Bridge

This Is Me

I am a...
Wonderful winger
Dog lover
Determined defender
Super swimmer
Superb singer
Enthusiastic educator
And finally...
Rough reader
This is me!

Edward Henderson (8)
St Mary's Catholic Voluntary Academy, Marple Bridge

This Is Me

My name is Raeya,
I really don't like hot weather,
My little brother is annoying,
But I love him and I hope he knows!
I really love it,
When it snows.
I'm brave and I'm bold,
But sometimes,
I'm scared of getting old.
I'm smart and I love art,
But one thing about my brother is that he always farts!
I don't like schoolwork,
It can be a bore,
I used to like schoolwork,
But not anymore!
I don't know what I'd do without my mom,
She's always there for me when things go wrong!
My dad is my hero,
Amazing is he!
I haven't written much, but this is me!

Raeya Banga (10)
St Michael's CE Primary School, Pelsall

This Is Me

Hi, I quite like hockey,
I like that I'm a happy boy,
I'm also funny,
Blue is my favourite colour.

I don't like mosquitoes on my neck,
I don't like spicy food,
I don't like it whenever my hair sticks up,
I hate spiders.

I don't eat mushrooms,
I am the best reader of all,
I don't like getting out of bed,
I hate going downstairs.

I love cats like me,
I am a cat that can land on my feet.
I don't like it when I have chillies on my plate,
If I have celery in front of me,
I will not touch it.

This is me.

Connor Knights (9)
St Michael's CE Primary School, Pelsall

This Is Me

T he best meal is Greek food,
H aving good thoughts about family,
I am a superstar!
S titch is my favourite character,

I love dancing,
S wimming is my strength,

M y favourite colour is blue,
E verlasting friendship, I'm so lucky, I have the best friends ever!

Anna-Maria Kamenou (9)
St Michael's CE Primary School, Pelsall

This Is Me

I am a galloping spirit,
I love animals,
Bambi is my favourite horse,
I am as blonde as a hay bale,
I play clarinet - as squeaky as mice,
I am adventurous like astronauts,
This is what I do,
I am as happy as a flower,
I play with dogs,
Some dogs chase squirrels, some do nothing,
This is what I do.

Elsie-May Witton (9)
St Michael's CE Primary School, Pelsall

This Is Me

T he game I play is football
H ate hockey, never liked it
I don't mind basketball, quite good at it
S port is my favourite

I 'm very fast, I win every race
S peedy like a cheetah

M any dreams about a dog
E nd up with my parents saying no.

Harry Pickersgill (9)
St Michael's CE Primary School, Pelsall

This Is Me

I am kind to friends and family,
I am stronger than a gorilla,
I am as fast as a sperm whale while swimming,
I am an exceptional player on my game,
I could be a talented trumpet player,
I don't like football or basketball,
My family and friends inspire me to be a better person,
This is me.

Oliver Boyd (9)
St Michael's CE Primary School, Pelsall

This Is Me

T alented at football
H olidays as peaceful as a bird
I am healthy
S ometimes I am silly

I am as fast as a cheetah
S ea is really blue

M cDonald's is my favourite
E xcited when I see my dog.

Teddy Park (9)
St Michael's CE Primary School, Pelsall

This Is Me

I am as tall as a giraffe,
I am as fast as Flash in my boots,
I am a fantastic striker,
I am a kind person inside,
I am as strong as a tiger,
I am brave,
My hair is brown like the branch of a tree.

This is me.

Theo Graham (9)
St Michael's CE Primary School, Pelsall

This Is Me

I am like a cat in goal,
I am as strong as an ape,
I am as friendly as a Labrador,
My favourite footballer is Martinez,
My favourite team is Aston Villa,
My favourite animal is a dog.

This is me.

Max Johnson (9)
St Michael's CE Primary School, Pelsall

This Is Me

Black,
My favourite shade,
I am brave like a lion,
Red,
My favourite colour,
I like to game.

Logan Cannon (9)
St Michael's CE Primary School, Pelsall

All About Me

I am a super defender and striker.
I am good at basketball.
I am a football lover.
I am a tennis lover.
I am a basketball lover.
I am very curious and adventurous.
I am a Greece lover.
I am strong, brave and intelligent.
I am fun.
I am kind.
I am respectful.
I am honest.
I am nice.
I am loving.
I am very bold and friendly.
I am my family lover.
I am a speed lover.
I am an Arsenal lover.
This is me.

Samuel Adams (9)
St Teresa's Catholic Primary School, Ashford

This Is Me

I like my family.
I'm a gamer.
I love loom bands.
I'm a fan of IShowSpeed and Blackpink.
I love reading.
I love school.
I love going on holiday.
I love me and you should love yourself!

Gabriella Muthaiga (8)
St Teresa's Catholic Primary School, Ashford

This Is Me

I am a good rider.
I am a good bee.
I am a nice drawer.
I am a learner.
I am a nice sister.
I am a nice designer.
My hair is as brown as a branch.

Jennifer James (8)
St Teresa's Catholic Primary School, Ashford

Loren Harvey

L oren is my name and I live in Stromness
O utdoors is my favourite place to play
R ed, pink and purple are my favourite colours
E lla is my sister and Thorfinn is my brother
N etball is one of the sports I play

H arvey is my last name
A nd I love puppies and dogs
R eading is one of my favourite things
V iolin is my thing
E very Tuesday I go to Gymnastics
Y ou now know a bit about me.

Loren Harvey (9)
Stromness Primary School, Stromness

This Is Me

T rampolining with my friends is fun
H ere is why: they're really annoying but funny
I like cooking and paddleboarding
S ee my glossy blue eyes and golden locks of hair

I love my cats and my hamster
S eriously

M y name is Halle
E very day, I play with my friends.

Halle Dixon (10)
Stromness Primary School, Stromness

This Is Me

All the time, I'm with my dog,
Laughing when my sister fell off the chair,
I'm on YouTube a lot of the time,
One of my favourite hobbies is Fortnite,
All the time, my sister annoys me.

Alysha Sutherland (10)
Stromness Primary School, Stromness

This Is Me

I love my hamster named Biggles Bee,
She makes me giggle with glee,
I love eating gooey chocolate,
Although I can't bake,
I love playing with my friends,
We hide in our secret den.

Willow Beckett (8)
Tanners Wood Junior Mixed And Infant School, Abbots Langley

About Me

Dino lover
Glasses wearer
Boba lover
Sweet stealer
Happy smiler
Rain lover
Brown eyes
Tealby member
Talented writer
Cricket lover
Water hater
Mosquito hater
Crisp lover
Car lover
Craft lover
Wasp hater
School lover
Maths hater.

Hattie Pouncey (9)
Tealby School, Tealby

Me

I am a...
Tennis player
Sand hater
Game winner
Sporty swimmer
Dino lover
Glasses wearer
Quad racer
Bike rider.

Henry Worrell (8)
Tealby School, Tealby

This Is Me!

Football lover
Goal saver
Medal winner
Ball kicker
Football player
Pitch lover.

Grace Worrell (8)
Tealby School, Tealby

A Recipe Poem About Me

Gather fun and ice cream and stir
Then pour it into a bowl.
Dash a chunk of ham pizza.
Stir in a chunk of ham pizza.
Pour in a bucket of sunlight.
Put in a roomful of games.
Blend in a bowlful of smiles.
Add a pinch of energy.
Put in the oven for 20 minutes.

Winston Wahlers
The Discovery School, West Malling

A Recipe Poem About Me

First, gather a pinch of trust.
Stir in a teaspoon of pretzels.
Season it with a jar of chocolate.
Add a slab of sushi.
Pour in a jar of sour sweeties
And a boxful of drinks.
Blend in a pound of milkshakes
Then a tray of fun.

Aliyah Bashorun (8)
The Discovery School, West Malling

Gone To University

M issing
Y ou

S pecial person
I nspiration
S upportive
T alented
E ver loving
R eliable.

Fraser Chapman (9)
Thornton Primary School, Thornton

This Is Me!

L ove Stitch
A pples are delicious
Y ummy! Mum's macaroni!
L ovely long hair
A mazing at gymnastics.

Layla McIntyre (7)
Townhill Primary School, Townhill

This Is Me!

E die is excellent
D aylight dream
I love cats
E very day, I'm happy!

Edie Martin (7)
Townhill Primary School, Townhill

This Is Me!

D aring
E xcellent
C aring
L ovely
A wesome
N ice.

Declan Lawlor (8)
Townhill Primary School, Townhill

This Is Me

Ecstatic when playing football on a cold Sunday morning,
Delighted when I slide tackle and win the ball,
Giddy when I get to go to a water park,
Overjoyed when I go on my bike for a bike ride through the forest.

Glum when I lose a game on FIFA,
Down when I can't play games on my PlayStation,
Sorrowful when my opponent scores a last-minute winner in a FIFA match,
Miserable when I can't play outside.

Furious when I don't get to go out on my bike,
Irritated when I don't do well in something,
Fuming when Southampton lose a football match,
Livid when teenagers think they're hard in their balaclavas.

Terrified when I go on a roller coaster,
Horrified when there's a big spider,
Petrified when I see a large snake,
Afraid of getting rejected by something.

Kian Wilson (10)
Waterside Primary School, Hythe

Christian Kwan

C aring to others.
H elpful, yes that's me.
R eally like to be creative.
I love to write stories.
S ushi is delicious.
T alented.
I ce cream is my favourite dessert.
A nimals are fascinating.
N ever mean to people.

K arate is one of my topics after school.
W atercolours are amazing to me.
A fraid of beasts.
N ice to teachers.

Christian Kwan (7)
Wetherby Kensington, London

Love To Play

W hen I play I play Guess Who?
I have a fast dog called Camron.
L ove my mom and dad.
L ove to play with them too.
I love new toys, they make me smile.
A nd my favourite things are stuffies.
M y grandparents are very nice.

William Garton (7)
Wetherby Kensington, London

Awesome Me

S uper at running.
E xcellent at sports.
B rilliant at jumping.
A mazing athlete.
S uper intelligent.
T errific.
I maginative.
A wesome.
N ever gives up.

Sebastian Fernandez (7)
Wetherby Kensington, London

What Am I?

What am I?

I wander in the African savannah,
Roaming in the tall grass,
I proudly stand,
Roaming the land I pass.

My body is covered in brown fur,
My hooves a dark shade of black,
My horns are long and curved,

I'm a grazer, so I can eat green,
On the savannah grass I feast,
In a large herd I travel,
To ensure my safety at least.

My life is not easy,
There are many dangers around me,
But I have the strength and courage,
To survive and still be free.

Answer: Wildebeest/gnu.

Marcus Kipps (10)
Willington School, Wimbledon

I Am

I am passionate about our planet,
I love all creatures great and small,
I am Chelsea's greatest superfan,
I love belting a football,
I am cheeky with my brother,
I love cooking with my sister too,
I am as playful as a dolphin,
I love bouncing like a kangaroo,
My hair has shades of autumn
And is wavy like the sea,
My eyes are aqua-blue,
This is me.

Fin Pittam (8)
Willington School, Wimbledon

A Recipe For My Best Friend, Riley

First, gather a bag full of joyfulness and laughter,
Stir in sports and a stone full of energy,
Season with fantastic times together,
Add a pinch of jokes that you will never forget,
Pour in an Earth full of gaming,
And a box of the strongest men in the world,
Blend skills, smiles, sweetness and exciting surprises,
Then warm gently by sitting on his bed and eating McDonald's.

Marlee Smith (9)
Ysgol Penmorfa, Prestatyn

A Recipe For My Dog, Roxy

First, gather cuteness and loyalty,
Stir in a ball,
Season with kisses, tickles and games,
Pour in a tug rope to rag around and tasty treats,
Add a neverending supply of footballs,
And toys and her ball,
Blend barks and speed and walkies in the dark,
Then warm gently by coming to cuddle me in my bed,
This is Roxy.

Riley Peacock
Ysgol Penmorfa, Prestatyn

A Recipe For My Bestie, Amber

First, gather generosity and funniness,
Stir in a cup of tea and a phone call with Amber,
Season with kindness and friendliness,
Add a pinch of Roblox and happiness,
Pour in excitement and success,
Blend sweetness, hope and effort,
Then warm gently with a big hug with a good friendship.

Willow Jones (9)
Ysgol Penmorfa, Prestatyn

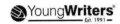

Young**Writers** Est. 1991

YOUNG WRITERS INFORMATION

We hope you have enjoyed reading this book – and that you will continue to in the coming years.

If you're the parent or family member of an enthusiastic poet or story writer, do visit our website **www.youngwriters.co.uk/subscribe** and sign up to receive news, competitions, writing challenges and tips, activities and much, much more! There's lots to keep budding writers motivated!

If you would like to order further copies of this book, or any of our other titles, then please give us a call or order via your online account.

Young Writers
Remus House
Coltsfoot Drive
Peterborough
PE2 9BF
(01733) 890066
info@youngwriters.co.uk

Join in the conversation!
Tips, news, giveaways and much more!

YoungWritersUK **YoungWritersCW** **youngwriterscw**

Scan me to watch the This Is Me video!